While this may seem at first like a rant against politicians and bureaucrats, I am really only speaking out against how apathy has allowed our government to devolve. After all, bureaucrats are voters too — and there's a lot of them.

There's no malice intended here. There is concern though, that we are being manipulated, not led.

All I'm trying to do is propose a way to make political manipulation a useless endeavor and to help some, as yet, unknown leaders emerge from the oppression of an apparent creeping and global Socialist agenda. Please read on. It's only 75 pages.

C3

THE INDEPENDENT TEA PARTY

CONTENTS

Thanks to my favorite bureaucrat, KH, who was kind enough to do some proof-reading for me and also get two-cents in where I was sounding too much like Atilla The Hun.

The Three Party System

The Independent Tea Party

Federal

State

Local

No thinking person needs much convincing that we've wasted a whole year with a Congressional stalemate over ideological approaches to how this country will be governed and run by legions of politicians who mostly have only one real aim — to be reelected and to retain a cushy job.

They've all heard over the years, that we think they should have to follow the same rules we do and have to live with the social benefits all their constituents do. Nothing ever changes though — does it? There have been attempts to add constitutional amendments addressing practically every ill we face today, but back-room dealings always grant whatever lobbyists push and whatever is needed to keep the taxpayer uninformed and irrelevant. If the President and Governors are limited to two terms, why aren't all elected officials. They're like fish and visiting relatives who should all move on after awhile because they start to stink.

It's Now or Never

We are at a unique crossroad and have the opportunity to effect real change in the elected government's way of doing business — our business. There's been so much grass roots upheaval and consternation at this country's predicament that we are coming together in a movement that can forever change the way we are served.

When Sarah Palin first appeared in the National limelight, she immediately sparked an "Its about time" feeling. She embodied an anti-Politically Correct, "say it like it is" emotion repressed in our jaundiced outlook after years of Washington insiders doing what they damn well pleased, without regard for the taxpayers who were steered into putting them there by skillful political marketeers.

It's probably fortuitous that she wasn't elected to the VP spot. Along with many others, I felt she wasn't ready, but that she holds immense potential for 2012, if she learns about the world beyond Alaska and exhibits the leadership we all hope and think she might have. There are still puzzling questions about her path to this perceived goal.

Nonetheless, her Cowboy approach has awakened the wild west feeling in us about politics and that the white hats and Joe The Plumber can win this time around. Everybody who has been voting against a candidate, never *for* one because they all stink, now has been emboldened to get up and go to Tea Party meetings and speak out. Most Americans have never done that.

Heretofore, complacency has let our political system

devolve into shameless manipulation of every outcome. This has become the norm in American politics and what has emboldened former "Who cares — what can I do?" voters to say, "Enough of this crap". That's why the Tea Party movement is going to redefine our politics.

The stalemate of two parties at impasse should be a thing of the past with a third party in the negotiations. The platform of the Independent Tea Party has yet to be defined, and that is the main reason for this writing. They haven't decided to be a united party yet. I intend to make my point as to what I think most people feel about our position in the world, and what goals we should be endorsing. I'll explain this position and offer it as a possible starting point for a 2012 Tea Party Platform.

Why do we need anybody?

If you ask a politician they say, "Well, it's a global economy and, we want to foster Democracy around the world. We have to help the poor people in third world countries. We have to make sure Iran and North Korea don't nuke their neighbors and we, we, we, we, we . . . . ."

How many Americans have you talked to that really give a damn about the global economy, the UN or for that matter, the rest of the world? Did any politician ever ask you personally, how you feel about these issues?

Rumors are, we're just now getting ready to send US Special Forces into Somalia to deal with the al-Qaeda pirates raising hell in nearby shipping lanes in the Indian Ocean and the Gulf of Aden. As you'll probably remember that's where we lost 16 Special Forces Americans, dramatized in the movie, "Blackhawk Down". You'll also remember that it took the current PC administration four days to make up its mind to shoot back at the pirates when an American flagged cargo vessel was attacked.

I believe US Coast Guard corvettes should accompany flotillas of US shipping through pirate infested waters until some UN mandate is debated and a force sent into Somalia. They need to be taken completely over to eliminate genocide and al-Qaeda in that area. I believe that we have done enough in that part of the world. Let the European Union's forces make it a new piece of their European influence.

A plan

— Without reasonable, measurable goals and *flexible* plans to achieve them, failure is the usual consequence, amply demonstrated by our recent forays into the Health Care morass. This outcome has been proven time and again, by the lack of individual achievement, by volunteer organizations squabbling incessantly rather than achieving, by Corporations foundering under huge restructuring gaffs and by whole nations with America as a prime example, not accomplishing anything worthwhile, just reacting to immediate needs, and all due to *"No Goal and/or No Plan".*

Our recent health care wasted year, amply demonstrates this shortcoming. A comprehensive and all encompassing plan might have brought it to a majority vote consensus. The notion might be a good thing for all Americans, but what was approved was too lopsided and just as important, is the fact that they schmoozed it through using smoke and mirrors. Americans are finally paying attention and they don't like how they're being screwed.

What are America's goals? What are the plans to achieve them? Does anybody know the answers to those questions? None and None and No would be my guess.

Broad goals should be emblazoned on our souls, our edifices, our money and taught from pulpits and classrooms. Specific goals are more difficult to define due to ideologies, ethnicity and religious affiliation, but are as necessary as leaves are to a tree.

It is clear that America is sinking and that is largely due

to partisan foundering, uncontrolled special interest lobbying in every effort and elected officials not representing their constituents now and in the recent past.

We've decisively won wars and rehabilitated the vanquished where there was a goal and a plan, and have been mortified in Korea and Viet Nam and almost in Iraq where there was no plan initially to achieve a just goal.

With a lofty goal, a good plan and determined minds, we went to the moon. Our kids can't make change today or pinpoint Hawaii on a globe without Googling it. No Child Left Behind is a good and lofty goal, but the plan to get there also needs some urgent revision.

We've run short and paid exorbitant fuel prices, yet have massive untapped natural resources. Surely we can devise a plan to satisfy diverse goals such as protecting the environment and at the same time exploiting natural resources. Both goals are for the common good. Those goals and any other worthwhile goal for that matter can be achieved, but only with a good, *flexible* plan.

The first milestone is to define these overall goals as they pertain to America and Americans. *No consideration must be given at this point to if, or how, or how much — only what we want to achieve.* Once that list is complete and carved in stone, and printed on our money, plans to get there must be created.

AMERICA...AGAIN

<u>Goals</u>

Revamp Our Political System

Streamline Government

Redefine America's Global Posture

Complete Independence

Entitlements

Note: Add your own broad Goals

Now is the time

My diatribe here could go on forever. But we don't have forever to debate what's wrong. We've all got stories to tell and gripes about this and that. What we really have right now is probably the most unique and important opportunity of our political lifetime to try to make it all work better with less bickering, time wasted and with defined results. Now is the time when we must create the framework of the new *Independent Tea Party*. We must approach this next election with a list of goals to be won and outlines for the plans to win them.

The Republican party is hoping we don't form a new third party. I wonder why? Probably because they see their shot at regaining control of Congress again and perpetuating their ideals without having to go to war to get anything accomplished. *That is precisely why a third party if needed.* No one group or ideology should be able to completely dominate without having to reach compromises. Didn't we just watch this happen?

The current health care debates are illustrating what the perverted Congress is able to accomplish with gerrymandered rules and without regard for the people who pay their salaries when there are inadequate checks and balances.

None of the following will materialize without new thinking here.

Specific Milestones

I'm outlining specifics *I'd like to see* achieved and why. These may or may not be in line with yours, but my efforts here are a starting point to finally come up with a set of American goals to be achieved. I don't expect the Independent Tea Party to include me directly in their planning, but I surely want them to know how me and many of my acquaintances feel.

Each of my benchmarks are outlined in the next few pages and discussed in more detail later on, but all from my perspective. Please add your thoughts to mine. Maybe you could copy the pages after you've added your thoughts or changed mine, and pass them around to your friends to see if they are are in agreement with you. C'mon — talk it up!

Revamp Our Political System

▶ **Create a Third Party** — Many voters don't agree totally with either ideology and vote on the merits of the measure rather than the political orientation of the introducing party. How can you eliminate gridlock with only two voters?

▶ **Term Limits** — House politicians serve no more than one six-year term, ensuring full attention to their constituents. Senate politicians serve one eight-year term.

▶ **Line Item Veto** — *All Pork* goes into an annual Omnibus Bill in balanced budget *only if deficit = $0.* Line-item veto applies. Each bill stands alone with nothing attached.

▶ **Change the Rules** — Eliminate Congressional rules used to pervert the "Yes/No" aspect of voting, now subverted by special back-room dealing to enlist recalcitrant legislators.

▶ **Outlaw Lobbyist & Lobbying** to individual politicians – Only to congressional committees in session on C-Span.

▶ **Eliminate "BUYING" a political position** — Campaign reform; Federal, State & Local

▶ **Equal Application** — All laws, Entitlements, Mandates and Regulations must apply equally for elected officials and their constituents, — Federal State & Local.

▶ **Presidential Qualifications** — Candidates should be chosen based on certain qualifications, much like a Corporate CEO is, and only from Senatorial ranks.

▶

Streamline Government

▶ **Flat Federal & State Gross Income Taxes** — Dependents (- $5000 each), Flat on gross business receipts.

▶ **National Sales Tax** — Includes internet sales & is apportioned to states to cover school taxes & Federal mandates. State/local taxation for infrastructure only.

▶ **Consolidate Departments and functions** — Eliminate redundancy between departments and the regions within them.

▶ **Balanced Annual Budgets** – Zero Based budgeting requires each line item to be justified, rather than just seeking increases over the previous year's budget line item.

▶ **Eliminate Foreign Aid** if deficit remains. Must be included in current balanced budget resulting in $0 deficit.

▶ **National ID card** – Driving license – Carry Permit – Passport - health record etc.

▶ **Legalize drugs** – Create "Happy Hollow" communes where people can abuse themselves to their hastened death.

▶ **Strict Immigration Limits** through Ellis Island, as before. No benefits till becoming English speaking US citizen with an American sponsor and job.

▶

▶

Redefine America's Global Posture

▶ **Develop impregnable borders and "Star Wars" shield.**

▶ **Withdraw** from all Foreign Military Bases. Lessen involvement in the UN & NATO processes.

▶ **Use Torture Where Necessary** on terrorist, not uniformed soldiers. Rewrite Geneva Convention. Guantanamo symbolizes "Terrorist end-of-the-road."

▶ **Universal Service at 18** – Military 2 years or Civil 3 years.

▶ **Never Commit Troops** unless annexing territory

▶ **Dominance** — Reaffirm America as the leader of the world in Pure Research, Applied Research and Space dominance

▶

▶

Independence

▶ **Energy Independence** – Develop all resources and technologies. Sell surplus to the global market. Supply lines for strategic products end at US borders. We shouldn't have to import critical products that might be under the control of a potential adversary.

▶ **Manufacturing Independence** – Supply lines for strategic products end at US borders.

▶ **Agricultural Independence** – Supply lines for beef, dairy and basic produce end at US borders.

▶ **Financial Independence** — Eliminate the deficit. Return to the Gold Standard. Eliminate the Federal Reserve.

▶ **Invest in "Small Town USA"** – Incentivize family farms & small town USA, not cities, super stores and factory farms.

▶ **Buy American**

▶

▶

Entitlements

▶ **Birth to Death Medical Care** — US Clinics for *basic* care (family doctor), emergency & medications only. Personal insurance covers everything else including related medication.

▶ **Education** — K through 12 for every US Citizen child with vouchers for alternative and private schools. Grants for education in areas deemed necessary for strategic progress.

▶ **Social Security** — Trust fund IOUs recalled and locked by Constitutional Amendment.

▶ **Welfare** — Funds used by Welfare client are treated like a Student Loan that must be repaid. The duration for enrollment is predefined. Universal Service credited to this account.

▶

▶

The American Marque

▶ **Define what the name America means in the world**

▶ **Clarify what an American Tradition means**

▶ **Reestablish "Made in USA" dominance**

▶

If I don't see positive steps toward these goals, especially Term Limits, I'm going to push for a referendum on the 2012 ballots Nationwide, although that's not the best way to go.. Help me.

The following tirades are my thoughts on some of the preceding bulleted items — but in more depth. Most are no-brainers and most of my acquaintances agree.

Revamp US Political System

November, 1956 was my first presidential vote — Dwight Eisenhower. I voted for him in his second term, against Adlai Stevenson and when he had Richard Nixon as his VP. I wasn't involved in anything political in those days, but I seemed to always believe that business was the engine that drove the world. Heroes were Eisenhower, or business magnates like Henry Ford and Rockefeller, Andrew Carnegie, William Randolph Hurst — visionaries like Edison and Einstein, achievers like the Wright brothers, Glen and Armstrong. Today's heroes are overpaid sports figures, bare-midriff Hollywood tarts or little loud over-privileged Hollywood kids. Don't get me wrong. I don't have anything against them personally — but, what do they represent? Our American culture has become a vast hedonistic wasteland where achievement is only celebrated if its got big bucks or big tits attached.

Meanwhile the US is on a rapid downhill decline into mediocrity and socialism. I tried, back in the 70s and 80s, to do my part by becoming a Republican Committeeman, a lackey in big city machine-politics. It was always fun and always hard work getting the vote out. Being a Republican in Philadelphia was usually frustrating because we most always lost and when we did win, the jerk became a despised power broker who engineered back-room deals only representing his State Politician buddies, not me. Everybody was a fireman, a cop or a crossing guard — all Democrats (by unwritten decree).

I didn't vote for Obama because his politics — his Hollywood and Chicago cronies, are way too far left for me. I would have if he was more centrist, because he has leadership qualities seldom exhibited by career politicians, or so I thought. It seems clear now that he is being driven by forces most of us are very naive about.

He is the perfect commercial for learning how to speak in public (with a teleprompter). I firmly believe every student should have "required" public speaking classes. Caroline Kennedy lost out in her bid to continue in the Kennedy tradition I believe, partly because she didn't come across as a very polished speaker. Her name was the only qualification she thought she needed to fill a US Senate seat. That's all that would matter to most of the political dimwits in this country, or so her backers thought.

Obama today (3/2010), seems to have gone back on all his campaign rhetoric. However Obama is keeping true to his redistribution of my wealth and welcoming of all comers to US largess.

The July 4th 2009 Pocono (Pennsylvania), Record had a front-page article analyzing why voter turnout continually declines and the author correctly surmised the reason is that the contemporary American voter doesn't give a damn anymore. Previous votes didn't seem to change anything.

Everyone I talk to, no matter their professed political affiliation, all express the same withdrawal from a malfunctioning system — and from State and Federal legislators who do not work for you and I, but only to protect their political tenure.

They all have high paying positions, with lavish expense accounts, better health and retirement plans than any of their constituents; so why is it so hard to see their main motive is to keep milking their golden cow.

Partisan bickering at every level of our Government, produces nothing of real value; no simple school tax reform, just slots jammed down our throats at the State level, Medicare's overpriced prescription drug program — pork barrel projects that would never pass a vote on their own merits attached to every piece of major legislation. It's an ongoing litany of smoke and mirrors, with one sure result — reelection of self-serving politicians.

We have a president who seems elitist and arrogant and lately on both sides of every issue, trying desperately to say just what we all want to hear. Now he's for offshore drilling. Bet there's some hidden meaning in that reversal. We have a President who seems to be a lousy planner and worse, seems unable to eat humble pie (George Bush too), and admit mistakes and revise whatever dopey plan he might have had. Thank God term limits are imposed on that office. Even if another jackass schmoozes his way in, he's sure to be out in eight.

Does it seem that we will ever realize fair and intelligent legislation, a prosperous nation minding its own damn business, energy independence, closed borders with sane and strict immigration laws — a nation respected for its restraint and iron fist at the same time?

How can we turn this mess around?

The first step is to find a way to impose term limits on elected officials, bad and good. They're all "out" after one term. The good ones might be reelected after a term off, or could move to another elective office. The bad ones never reelected and out for good. Step two is for all of us to register "Independent Tea Party" for awhile to build a third party, so legislative gridlock might be lessened in the future.

The current Health Care fiasco is the best example of why we need a third party. One says "No". The other says "Yes", which equals gridlock and degenerates into back room arm twisting, special interest deals and bending of all the rules on a grand scale. Sometimes they seem to invent new rules, just for their own cause. They can't do that! The recent Health Care fiasco has been enlightening for Mr. & Mrs. John Q. Baby Boomer Public. Who could have imagined the depths of Government manipulation that goes on in our name?

Certainly none of our current crop of elected officials is going to vote himself out of a cushy, tenured job by opting for Term Limits. The only way I can see to bring that about is by voter referendum questions on Federal, State and local ballots. Does anyone have a better idea? I don't like referendums.

They all know that this American system of government, in its current state of partisan gridlock, is impossible to do anything within reason without years of infighting and selling of their souls to the other party's devil. Nothing ever gets done just on its merits, but only when earmarked or pork-barreled and is seldom what the public wants or needs. There are numerous examples of $600 toilet seats and bridges to nowhere, just to keep some political hack in his seat for another useless term. We didn't need the bridge and for sure we don't need the hack for another term, but guess what? His political machinery and the people who built the bridge will get him reelected again and again. America gets screwed again and again.

Line Item Veto

Every voter says this is needed. Why then, doesn't the president have it, or use it? Every Politician cringes when the subject comes up because that's the only way he keeps his job. They barter back and forth to secure each other's vote on a favorite piece of legislation. If the pork was eliminated from all legislation, each one might get a legitimate consideration on its merits, not on the fact that favors are owed. Some of the pork items have merit, but they are inconsequential when considered in comparison to a major piece of legislation. But, does anyone think the recent health plan would have ever passed if there were no pork favors included.

I'm proposing that pork spending be addressed in an *annual* Omnibus bill before the Congress and voted on, line item by line item. Implementation of those items approved must be deficit neutral.

This is in the same boat with term limits. They'll never vote to change it, so how do we do it for them?

Change the rules

Our new health plan legislation was only passed by twisting every available Democratic arm in the Congress and by bending legislative rules most of us never knew existed. What kind of way is that to do the business we sent them there to do for us? This is not just a Democratic tactic, but apparently has been going on without our paying attention for a long while, both parties. They knew we weren't paying any attention before, but that's changed now.

The current Parliamentary Procedures have too many loopholes, allowing determined manipulators to "Suspend The Rules" or subvert the essence of a rule to achieve an unpopular result. We've just seen this happen — somehow this must be prevented in the future.

Outlaw Lobbyist and Lobbying

Any advocate for something can be considered to be lobbying for it. I'm advocating a new "Independent Tea Party" but if I try to influence a Congressman by taking him on a fishing trip, that's bribery. I haven't convinced him, just used him and his constituents. to push a cause.

Lobbying is a legitimate way to bring information to people, to consumers and legislators, if done without coercion. TV commercials are a manufacturer lobbying his product to the masses. Washington's lobbyist know all the tricks and are as much of the legislative process today as you local rep is.

They do pass along valuable intelligence to the legislative process but should be restricted to lobbying the proper Congressional committee as a whole, in session and on C-Span. Strict and severe penalties should be levied on those who manipulate the system.

Campaign Reform

Saddam Hussein could even get elected here if he had the

money spent on this last election. Does the biggest war-chest equal the best candidate? Why should a rich man have a better shot at it than someone with more modest means. Why should power brokers be able to buy unsuspecting dupes votes?

There must be some way to control those who manipulate every outcome. Maybe the process has to be defined in strict guidelines, negating a shadow government or the world's bankers acting as puppeteer, pulling the strings necessary to control an outcome.

Equal Application

Maybe it's time for Amendment 28 to the Constitution.

"Congress shall make no law or regulation that applies to the citizens of the United States that does not apply equally to the Congress itself and to Legislative and Executive Offices. All previous laws and regulations granting special favor to elected officials shall be rewritten accordingly or abolished outright. This amendment shall apply to employees of all departments and branches of the US Federal Government here, abroad and elsewhere in the universe."

Presidential Qualifications

Political candidates who have the largest war chest usually win, regardless of qualifications. A business would never select a new president or CEO who didn't have management experience overseeing a similar business model. America has been selecting its Chief Executives from Congressional and Gubernatorial ranks with little thought about all the necessary credentials to manage it all.

Why not define the line of progression from local politics to State office, State Office to US House of Representatives and from there or State Governor to Senator in the US Congress where candidates for the Presidency are nominated, *only* from their ranks.

If you were a Human Resources person creating a list of credentials necessary for a prospective high-level Corporate position, at least one would detail expected past experiences relative to the job being applied for. If I was the recruiter, here's my list for US President:

► Former US Senator.

► Past Federal experience in Finance, Intelligence *and* Foreign Affairs.

► Former military – Company Grade Officer minimum.

► Past or present Business owner or Corporate Board Director.

► American born.

Streamline Government

Flat Federal & State Gross Income Tax

Personal income should have one deduction, dependents. Just for the sake of argument, that would be your kids and indigent parents or others dependent on you and wholly without income of any kind. Lets make that a $5,000 gross deduction for each.

Business income tax would be on Gross receipts, no deductions.

Consumption Tax on all products and services, with no exceptions. This is better than a Value Added Tax (VAT) which is invisible to the consumer, since it is built into the price of the product or service at each level of the manufacturing process. All you see is that a $2 product now costs $2.20. When a Consumption tax is added to your receipt as you check out of the store, the 20¢ is visible and a reminder of what your cost of government entitlements really are.

Income taxes at both Federal and State levels are used to run the government at each level. Consumption taxes are apportioned per capita to States to provide services such as Health Care, Hospice, Education and Social Security.

There would be only two taxes that the IRS would have to deal with. They could reduce the IRS payroll through attrition to 10,000 people Nationwide. You'd have 9,999 tax collectors and one guy with a computer running Quicken For Dummies.

Balanced Annual Budgets

These guys running the country's finances seem to have learned from me. I can tell them straight out — my way doesn't work. My Mammy and Pappy never had a credit card.

The "Beltway Boys" have the nerve to chide us constituents for running up our credit-card debt and not saving for the future. The Nanny government is supposed to take care of me. I'll give them the address to my Visa account. I've learned my lesson however and I live a very austere lifestyle now and intend to continue till my deficit is $0. I suggest the Beltway Boys gets on board with this notion for the next few years. My recent Visa statement now has a reminder that if I pay the minimum monthly payment, it'll only take me 30 years with no additional purchases. Add 60% to what I've been paying and it'll be done in three years.

Lets try some of these steps:

▶ Eliminate foreign aide until the deficit is reduced to $0 dollars. Restart it only if the annual budget is in balance and the deficit remains at $0. Freeze Federal hiring.

▶ Cap all Government salaries till parity is achieved with civilian salaries and deficit = $0.

▶ $0 based balanced budget each year. In other words, justify every proposed budget line-item.

▶ Caretaker status for foreign bases until $0 deficit.

▶ Until deficit = $0, reduce all UN & NATO commitments to "Let somebody else do it for a change" .

Consolidate

I'll use my personal experiences to illustrate some vexing problems. I got involved in April 2009 with the Census Bureau where I was a temporary Census Enumerator for a few months. I was told that I would remain on the Dept. of Commerce files as a Part Time Temporary Worker and would be recalled again when the actual census forms were mailed in March of 2010.

I was actually recalled twice. However I live and travel full time in my RV. When census time was approaching, I phoned and e-mailed the appropriate local and regional headquarters to tell them that I'd be staying temporarily in the Florida keys March through May of 2010 and offered my census services there during the expected busiest time. To most people that seems like a simple accommodation to me and to the census people in the Keys, because I was already in the system and trained.

I started in January with phone calls and e-mail to ask that my records be transferred to the responsible Florida office. My last conversation (3/6/2010) indicated that the records had to be Fed-X'd to Atlanta, so that I would be "visible" to the Homestead Florida census office. All this data and my work history were in a data base in the Philadelphia Region. It took them two months to finally figure out how to get my records from Harrisburg, PA to Homestead, FL. By the time this all transpired, I believe I was too late. I didn't get the job???

Why isn't the data instantly available to the other region? The internet goes between Philadelphia, Atlanta and to Homestead Florida I bet. I'll also bet there's 200 humans in that chain of responsibility, probably 198 of them not necessary for this simple task. It is unfathomable that data can't be moved just with one key-stroke, by just one person. What gives? Do we really need legions of bureaucrats, all afraid or too incompetent to make a decision. Fix the data-base to be visible across regions to provide instant service, and eliminate those 198 useless, well paid civil servants.

To further illustrate bureaucratic idiocy, I am now and have been a Volunteer for the Department of the Interior at National Wildlife Refuges and have, because of my past work background, been recruited to work in their offices on their computers creating Power Point presentations and archiving the extensive photographic records of the Flora & Fauna that they protect.

Understandably, working on Government computers would require security clearances. To get this certification, I believe the Government hires an outside contractor, who does a security and background check of the prospect. I told the Interior Department that all this had just been done in April 2009 by the Dept of Commerce for the Census Bureau job. Wouldn't you think this would greatly simplify and speed up the process? I'm taking bets that they did it all over again in July 2009. I wonder how much taxpayers were charged to do it a second time?

I've been under the care of the VA for many years. Since my lifestyle has changed and I now move around from place to place as a full time RV resident without a sticks and bricks home anywhere. Getting VA checkups and treatment requires me to reregister wherever I happened to be. I had a family emergency requiring me to fly to Miami on a moment's notice. I forgot my pills and since I was going to be there for about four days, I felt I'd croak too if I didn't get some.

I went to the Miami VA to get a four day supply to hold me over. The guy who checked me in could see my records from the Wilkes Barre, Pennsylvania VA Medical Center on his computer in Miami, but had to set me up with a doctor there to fill the order. This in effect, required me to transfer from Pennsylvania to Florida. It took at least two hours of their time and It seems like the same problem is prevalent no matter which government entity you are dealing with. I suspect the same thing is what gets between the FBI, CIA, NSA and the myriad other intelligence agencies, recently evidenced by the terrorist who tried to blow up his jock on an incoming flight.

I believe I could quite easily come up with a plan to eliminate most of these "Not invented here" idiosyncrasies of US databases and all the unnecessary bureaucracy attendant to following the rules and regulations. I wonder if I could work a deal to keep just .001% of all the money I could save them?

How much do you want to bet that there is a Human Resources Organization in every Federal Department, Division, Region and outhouse? Why?

I'll bet that there are a hundred three letter intelligence groups, such as FBI, CIA, NSA, ATF, ICE, TSA, Homeland Security (oops), plus the military which has its own intelligence groups in every branch. We all heard about lack of coordination, not sharing critical info in a timely manner, redundant operations, etc..

They have almost duplicate missions in some cases, with geography as the only difference, such as the hometown FBI and the CIA in the rest of the world. How much duplication do you think there is? They'll never admit to it trying to protect their turf. The only way that'll ever change is for the President to get all the three-letter head guys together and start firing them, one at a time, until they get the message, "Consolidate".

Google this link:

http://www.usa.gov/Agencies/Federal/All_Agencies/index.shtml

There are 15 major departments (Justice, Defense etc..), each with numerous Agencies, Bureaus, Committees ad-nauseam. I'll wager that most of them could be reduced to two desks -- boss and secretary.

National ID Card

Use current technology to develop a National ID Card that has all pertinent information about the individual carrying it. This could include:

▶ National driving license listing operator class and restrictions if any..

▶ Auto Insurance Carrier information

▶ Federal Firearm Concealed Carry Permit.

▶ Passport

▶ Medical alerts, contacts and Insurance status, i.e.: VA - Medicare - Private Insurance Carrier.

Legalize Drugs

Create "Happy Hollow" communes where residents can abuse themselves to their hastened death. The United States spends billions at least, trying to control the use and availability of illegal drugs. They could go a long way toward putting the suppliers out of business and cutting down on the crimes resorted to in the name of "needing a fix". These Communes could be equipped with the best of medical treatment and counselling.

The entrance fee is sterilization and a two year commitment to work there and to clean themselves up. Failure extends your commitment or leads to jail.

Alien Invasion

It seems that there are only a few countries left that have preserved their heritage and tradition. They seem to stay out of the limelight — away from conflict. They also seem to not give a damn much about what's going on in the rest of the world. There doesn't seem to be a large influx of other cultures trying to take them over. Or, maybe they've been assimilated more readily into the host' way of doing things, or maybe they are under strict guidance to, "Do it our war or take a hike back to where you came from".

The US has millions of illegals swimming in or jumping border fences, trying to meld into the background here. We tend to take care of them because our government is a nanny state. There are large populations of Mexicans, Haitians, Koreans and Russians, many Chinese, Vietnamese and Middle Eastern expatriates. Most of them are here legally. We must insist they become American, not Chinese American, African American, Mexican American — or get out.

Not listed above are the majority of European settlers who've come here over the years, and who have joined cultures with one language, assimilated their ideals into what we call America. These people are joined together by a desire to be one nation. Different parts of town harbor ethnic roots, but everybody eventually learns to speaks English on the street and in business. They don't try to globalize America. They want to be part of our America.

There's parts of Philadelphia where the street signs are in Korean. There are parts of Miami where no one speaks English. Some city schools have classes taught in Spanish for the kids because nobody at home speaks proper english. Recognizing Ebonics caused the Oakland, California School Board to drop that like a hot potato, due to a Nationwide outcry against Black English being taught. Oakland clarified their position, but it clearly fired up those who don't want a multicultural nation, but a nation where many cultures can assimilate into one.

Somehow that concept has waned in the latter half of the 20th Century until today, going from one end of a major city to the other is like going from one country to another.

A puzzling aspect of this diversity is the way the Chinese have managed to have a "Chinatown" in every major city in the world. Their home away from their homeland is accepted willingly for several reasons, I think. They are always there, but never demanding. They are always self sufficient, usually good neighbors and industrious businessmen. They don't force their culture on others and yet they have assimilated worldwide with no controversy. I don't believe we've ever made any concessions to their ethnicity or special education curriculum to help them. They always seem to be good citizens and all their kids speak American English, clearly.

Illegal aliens of every stripe have weedled themselves into American society and consciousness to the point where we are supporting them now and the damned government is trying to give them amnesty, so we can keep supporting their illegal needs legally. I have nothing against any of them personally, only in how they have learned how to work our increasingly Socialist country to the point that they are taxing our overextended resources, patience and resolve.

Past US Presidents had the courage to send them back. In the 1930s Herbert Hoover repatriated over a million Mexicans even though 60% of them were US Citizens. I'm not advocating that, because the Mexican is usually a good citizen and they are hard workers. In 1954 President Eisenhower instituted what was called "Operation Wetback" where illegal Mexicans were sent back in trains and boats way down into Mexico and all done with less than two thousand Border Patrol agents. A million went back, 650,000 voluntarily. I bet if you look into your kids Politically Correct history books, these pieces of our history are not widely discussed, if at all. An excellent internet article can be found at this link:

I don't know what prompted it, but politicians in 1965 eliminated the annual 100,000 quota of legal immigrants into the US. I believe at that time, they had to have a sponsor here and had to have a job and also had to learn English and some of our history before becoming a Naturalized American citizen.

That seemed to work OK. Entering this country through New York harbor and Ellis Island is one of those traditions I talked about earlier. Why did that change? Wikkipedia states that it was political maneuvering back in the Roosevelt era to allow the uncontrolled influx with the promise of citizenship in order to generate votes. Why do you think the Presidency then, was reduced to two terms after he passed on? Gee Willikers! Do you think this is happening today?

The following statistics from the CIS (Center for Immigrant Studies) are quoted from an article written 2/11/09 by Ron Livingston

"$11 to $22 billion is spent on welfare to illegal aliens each year.

Illegal households only pay about one-third the amount of federal taxes that legal households pay.

Illegal households create a net fiscal deficit at the federal

level of more than $10 billion a year.

If given amnesty, this number could grow to more than $29 billion.

$1.9 billion dollars a year is spent on food-assistance programs such as food stamps, WIC and free school lunches for illegal aliens.

$1.6 billion is spent on the federal prison and court system for illegal aliens.

$2.5 billion dollars a year is spent on Medicaid for illegal aliens.

About 21 percent of the population of U.S. prisons is classified as "noncitizens" from Mexico, Colombia, Cuba and the Dominican Republic."

A possible solution might be to immediately cease all welfare programs for illegals, but give them 5-year temporary Green work cards and a place in line at Ellis Island, where they must pass the required steps to becoming a citizen, including paying taxes and into the the normal entitlements. Prohibit further immigration until this green card crop is either naturalized or repatriated.

Redefine America's Global Posture

Mind your own business

Somewhere in the last 232 years this country has gotten the notion that it should tell everybody else how to live their lives. If your neighbor doesn't have enough food for his kids, do you share your larder with him? Maybe — once. How about the drug addicts over on the next block? Do you go over there and help them clean up or do their wash? Bet not, especially if they're different than you are.

As a nation, we've butted into conflicts all over the globe. It usually starts with insertion of some training forces and then Special Forces, long before the media thinks it's significant enough to headline a new involvement. Maybe it's sanctioned by the UN or NATO, but not in a newsworthy sense. I believe I read that Special Forces are going to make an effort in Somolia where pirates are trying to rule the high seas there in the Gulf of Aden and the Indian Ocean. Why us?

We've maintained a presence in every vanquished nation, and in some we're going to vanquish if the do-gooders have their way. These foreign bases not only cost a bundle to man and maintain, but are becoming unnecessary with today's technology. Look at how well we are prosecuting the Afghanistan conflict from drone control right here in the US. Air Force drones are launched over there, but controlled by satellite from right here in the good 'ole USA by kids who grew up playing "World of Warcraft" on their parents computer.

Piss me off and you __will__ pay.

Would this country ever have risen to the top by "Turning The Other Cheek"? I believe our top came when Germany and Japan were neutralized and then refined in our image in 1945. We jerked around in Korea, playing tag across an imaginary line that we're still policing 53 years later. If we'd have obliterated Pyongyang like we did Dresden and Tokyo, would North Korea be a problem today? If we leveled Hanoi, would we have gotten kicked out of Saigon?   Since we did decide to go to war, why didn't we fully occupy Iraq and Afghanistan, and then mandate workable governments like we did after WWII? An even bigger question is why were we in all those places in the first place? If it's worth putting boots on the ground, then it should be a total and complete victory with the end result looking like the 51st State.

We'd have to have a large standing Military to do those things, but that's easy if you have Universal Military Service. This might also help to mitigate some of the unemployment and border problems. Modify the Posse Comitatus rules and line our borders with this committed standing Army, facing out until *__only__ Congress votes to send any force onto foreign soil*.

Torture — or not?

A recent episode of the TV thriller "24" had Jack Bauer saving good guys and eliminating the bad ones as usual, but the undercurrent, the theme running throughout was, "How far do you go to get information"?

In this episode, he did all the things necessary to get life-saving information. What he did was, to his mind, expedient and necessary to save innocent people. The Geneva Convention wouldn't have allowed any of his tactics in the name of playing fair with your enemy. There's been great uproar on the Politically Correct front over harsh treatment of prisoners and against "inhumane" methods to extract information from terrorists. While I believe the Geneva Convention protects combatants in uniform; it was never intended to protect non-uniformed spies and terrorists.

Our non-uniformed terrorist adversaries never deferred to those conventions as they beheaded uniformed soldiers in front of television cameras. War in itself is inhumane and any rational person would do all in their power to help stop it. Why do PCs care what the rest of the world thinks about our tactics? Winning the conflict in the fastest possible time with the smallest number of US casualties is what counts, not what Europe thinks.

John McCain is against torture because he was a **uniformed** victim of it in North Vietnam. We adhered to the Geneva Treaty, the North Vietnamese didn't. The North Koreans didn't, back in the 50s. How do you get needed information from your adversaries? Do you just sit there and say, "Well, we can't go after his buddies, because we don't know where they are and we can't hurt him because his mommy might get mad at us". Or do you pull out his fingernails, feed him pork chops and water-board him until he pukes the answers?

Senator McCain and his POW compatriots deserve our admiration and every accolade and thanks this nation can muster for them, but we're not talking about them, in uniform.

Did the CIA use all the tricks in its bag in Viet Nam? My guess is that's where water-boarding was invented. Back in the mid 1950's the American press was getting on the US Air Force for torturing its airmen at their Stead Air Force Base Survival School near Reno, Nevada. The "POW compound" there, was part of their combat survival training — knowing what you face is necessary information if you're ever caught. Torture is nasty! The PC liberals of the time eventually got the Air Force to stop the training. I was there — what a shame.

Star Wars Shield

Ronald Regan was way ahead of the Political elite, and his futuristic approach to American safety went over the heads of the Congress of the day. We've come a long way with mostly unfunded technological implementation of Beamed Weapons and now seem to have the ability to melt things from space. This technology was perfected without any major emphasis or funding like Kennedy's moon efforts had.

With a dedicated commitment, we could be walled in by a laser fence nobody would venture to penetrate. Does any thinking adult believe our satellites are rolling around the heavens without some protections? I'll bet all the military versions have laser cannon protection now . . . . . could be even more advanced. I also believe they have unadvertised offensive capability. We'd be up the creek if some of the bad guys started taking pot-shots at them. Maybe they already have?

Withdraw

We have US troops stationed worldwide, most at military bases long established and all leftovers from previous conventional-warfare conflicts. As battle tactics evolve and become more "Remote" with drone technology and beamed weapons from near space, we no longer need standing forces strategically positioned. We have a devastating, invisible, nuclear deterrent under the surface of every sea and ocean. Let our universal Army man the homeland borders and be mobile enough to be in battle anywhere on earth in 24 hours.

Foreign bases should be manned with only caretaker forces to keep everything in readiness should we need to put "Boots on the ground" there. The "Star Wars" scenario was premature maybe in Reagan's time, but it's not now. I read there is research and testing now at Area 51, I believe, on the use of crew-less drone cargo airplanes by UPS and FedEx? Why not?

Our support of the UN has been mostly a futile exercise over the years. America is almost always the major "Boots on the Ground" in every UN effort. We're always too anxious to save the world. Without our support the UN might just begin to take ownership of their mandate. Without the US effort and support the UN is nothing so far. Nobody pays attention to their dictates, unless we do it for them. Why don't we take a back seat there for ten years? If they begin to exercise their mandate, then maybe the US can take an equal, active role. Maybe the US could form a special American Blue helmeted UN force as part of Universal Military Training mandates, a token force to be used as the UN needs it, and just to keep our foot in the door.

Dominance

America used to lead the planet when technology and innovation were discussed. Today's global economy has lifted our neighbors sights and education up until they equal and in many cases surpass us today. We've invented and discovered most of today's technology and yet we don't anymore, nor do we produce most of it today. We enjoy the labors of today's entrepreneurs and big business, but they are not so much American anymore. The automobile industry is a shambles because of capitulation to ruinous union control. The steel industry is practically nonexistent today in this country partly for the same reasons. We invented nuclear power, but today we only have a few power reactors, compared to other countries. We have immense mental and natural resources, untapped. Our kids are not competing with Indian, Chinese and Japanese kids. I believe I lamented earlier about at least a third of all software developers today have front and back names we can't even pronounce.

In my former Corporate business career I worked with numerous Green-Card Electrical and Com-Si engineers, all top notch in their fields and all good people who are products of their educational systems and who have the drive to succeed, not like us in our welfare, semi solialist American way. A large standing Military might do several things:

▶ **Protect our borders from drug traffic & illegal aliens.**

▶ **Provide useful jobs for America's youth.**

▶ **Provide generous grants for quality service and low interest student loans based on length of service to** reassert young American's dominance.

▶ Provide an "Immediate Strike Force" .

▶ Provide mandatory Associate Degree studies for downtime.

INDEPENDENCE

Energy

What does that mean? To me, the guy with an RV, camped in the desert with solar panels and a wind mill is truly independent — until he has to drive somewhere else. What does Energy Independence mean to America. We always seem to get light when we flip a switch. We always get a TV picture. Although the price has gone up for gasoline, we still seem to be able to go someplace. Higher fuel prices are raising our cost-of-living, but we still manage — at least for the immediate future.

Quick cosmetic fixes are baloney. Independence means we don't need anyone's help or overpriced barrels of crude. We shouldn't need to import gasoline, because we don't have enough of our own refining capacity. Colonial fires of independence are what created this Nation. Why are we so dependent on the rest of the world now?

Today's global economy means we are dependent on other Nations for many of our needs. As long as we're satisfied with the availability, price and quality, no one complains too much. But we don't control commerce outside our borders and therefore have various levels of satisfaction with that world commerce. Oriental electronics and automobiles are top shelf. Third world's clothes and shoes are in every closet. South American produce is as good as it gets. Foreign petroleum is in every car, and it works well.

There are kinks in this arrangement. We have no control over these purveyors of products we can't do without??? Free Trade agreements have eliminated taxing as a tool or economic weapon. We don't have free trade agreements with the oil cartels

(OPEC) who fluctuate the price of their product on the whim of a few bankers, oil potentates and Mullahs and who vote against us in 75% of UN issues.

We should develop US oil resources "full speed ahead", and at the same time, exploit all other energy sources (nuclear – wind – CNG – shale oil – coal – solar - bio-fuels and hydro), none needing to be invented and most readily available today. These steps are considered short term — five years.

Long term, a concerted all-out USA technological blitz should be to the development of new natural-resource-independent energy, akin to JFK's "man on the Moon in ten years" challenge. When accomplished, America can be the world's largest *exporter* of coal, oil and other energy technology, helping to eliminate the deficit.

We are well on the way toward that goal with current efforts in fuel-cell technology. There seems to be no better solution. The fuel is hydrogen, the simplest and lightest and most abundant element in the universe (atomic #1). There are no downsides to this solution, including the lack of pollutants — just that nasty old water dripping from the tailpipe. The goal here seems to be, "how do we make the solution affordable enough to park in your garage, how to develop the infrastructure to support it, and what to do for the industries supplanted by it. Ten years ought to do it.

Manufacturing

As you drive by another era's manufacturing ghost town, such as Bethlehem Pennsylvania, or the vast windowless manufacturing ghettos in once-great cities, what do you think of? "Isn't that a great place to put another useless mall? Where do all those people work now? Why are all those local stores boarded up?" Anybody know why?

Unions? Union work rules? A widget maker in this business climate has to stay competitive so that you'll buy his widget. Go to your nearest Home Depot, to the tools department and price a Milwaukee screw-gun and a Rigid or Makita version. The made-in-the-USA Milwaukee tool cost $200+, while the Rigid lists at $79. Everyone but the contractor will buy the $79 tool made in China or Japan. The contractor buys it because of perceived commercial quality maybe, but guess what, the $79 Rigid works great and you can buy three for the Milwaukee price.

The American manufacturer is being priced out of the market because he has to pay for counter-productive work rules and escalated wages and benefits. For those who don't know, "Work Rules" basically govern who can do what, where and when, in union controlled shops.

I was witness to an example of this, at Philco-Ford in the mid-70s. Few people recognize the Philco name these days — it disappearing into a union-caused catastrophe. I managed a force of computer technicians who fixed a warehouse full of Burroughs, room-filling computer mainframes for Philco-Ford. We were given an office/workshop area at their "C" street factory. They supplied two dismantled workbenches with six screw-in pipe-legs each. The union movers brought them, but wouldn't screw-in the legs. We had to wait till later in the day

53

for union "Millwrights" whose job it was to do such important technically difficult tasks. Me and a colleague screwed them all in, a five minute job, and we caught hell too, because it wasn't our job to do.

Don't get me wrong. Unions still have some benefit today. They generally keep tight control of their members, knowing that their days are numbered I guess. Union apprenticeship programs are still a great idea and usually turn out well qualified journeymen workers. A union trained electrician for instance always knows all the building code rules and time-tested techniques that "jack-of-all tradesmen" won't, or ignore. The problem is, how do we maintain the quality of American workmanship and products without the enormous difference in costs to produce them?

I have a young friend, living in the Florida Panhandle, who is planning to move back to his hometown, Chicago, so he can get a union roofers' job at $40 an hour. I don't begrudge him the exorbitant imbalanced wage, but how does roofing compare to a teacher's job?

Agriculture

Farming and its American way-of-life has declined in this last century to a factory-farm culture today. There's no doubt that there are economies of scale to be gained from this approach. It works very well and makes farm acreage more productive as a result, helping to compete with South American produce. But, something American is missing. Drive through once lush and vital farmland, where most farms were fifty to two hundred acres, and what do you see today? You see abandoned, fallow fields awaiting a condo developer. Nobody is there anymore. Should this way of life disappear in the name of progress? Should Mom & Pop grocery stores disappear in favor of a brand new mall with Wal-Mart and Home Depot eliminating 50 little stores in our once great little American towns, now boarded up.

I went into Meadville, Pennsylvania recently to have lunch. It's a typical northwestern PA small farm town, where well known and respected manufacturing of Channel-Lock hand tools takes place. You can buy a serviceable clone in Home-Depot for 1/3 the price. After the lunch hour, almost every storefront is locked up tight. Everybody shops at Wal-Mart now.

Somehow, everything that made America good and great has been replaced in the name of progress. I believe we give huge subsidies to factory farmers and tax-breaks to bring in Big-Box stores. Why not eliminate that in the name of preserving America and give the subsidies to farm co-ops where farm acreage is limited to 200 acres in one-family farms. Why not create Small-Town co-ops that receive subsidies and tax breaks to perpetuate a way-of-life and eliminate all tax breaks for the Wal-Mart's of the world who only serve to hawk products not made by American Moms & Pops.

I travel a lot, and this almost makes me cry. A favorite movie of mine is called, "Doc Hollywood". It's not Academy Award materiel for the Tinsel Town crowd, but for me it is, because our once-was America is so well represented in its satire. Its melodrama represents what once was America. "Grady" is what we should be subsidizing. It's the heart of America, not a hundred mile drive with no farmhouse anywhere in sight.

Financial Independence

My lifestyle will attest to the fact that I'm not a financial wizard. I do pay attention however, at least in the last few years. It seems we've been resorting to going to the Lottery every day to buy some false hope that tomorrow will "be my day". We've been visiting Vinny Chang (loanshark) and are on the brink of a visit from Vinnie's Boys.

My only culpability in this swindle is that I wasn't paying attention. Now I am. However, please tell the Boys to go break some knees in Washington DC — not mine. Try to find me. I'm out.

The position we're in today is helping us to make some bad decisions I fear. But, it still doesn't seem to sink into the nuts at the Treasury's printing presses.

Entitlements

Birth to death Medical Care

Entitlements are to Americans, just like apple pie — everybody wants some more. The Welfare Mom needs to feed yet another bastard. She stays just within the guidelines that get her monthly "Grub Stubs" and a medical card. It's now in their DNA. Old fogeys like me want complete medical coverage, including all the Viagra grandma can handle. They, including me again, want first rate home care and hospice. Everybody would like to have a free local doctor, but nobody wants socialized medicine either.

The country is divided after the Administration jammed through its version of what it thinks American Health Care should be. Historically this country has spent billions trying to help every other country in the world out of some quagmire or another, while similar problems exist here. One of the main reasons Obama's bill was so reviled is the lack of a viable plan to implement — one not adding to the debt load we already face.

The States already support medical services at hospital emergency rooms when the uninsured show up. The indigent and homeless show up there and wait long hours at their emergency room, just like its their personal family doctor.

The VA Medical system already has clinics all around the country that treat you just like a family doctor would. Beyond their charter, you are sent to a VA Medical Center, usually a grand and well equipped full-scope hospital.

Suppose the concept is expanded for all citizens over

the years as funds allow, and refer patients to expanded care that is covered by their personal paid up medical policy when necessary.

If they don't have a policy, too bad -- head to the nearest morgue. They have a place there where you can lay down. Any medications prescribed by the Federal clinic are provided by that clinic. If you've gotten something requiring elaborate testing and procedures, you'll need your own insurance. During most people's lives, they only visit their family doctor for broken legs, flu shots and wellness care advice.

Hospice care could be provided in the home only by Student nurses, Nurse practitioners and Interns honoring their commitment to three years of Universal Service. If you or your kids want or need something more, then again, private insurance is the answer.

The idea of service at Federal clinics might be fostered for all nurses and medical students as part of their formal medical training. Every hospital would have an emergency room attached, but under the control and funding of the US government. It would be relegated to true emergencies, not like today where it is the uninsured's family doctor.

Education

When I went to Catholic grammar school in the late 40's, the good Nuns ran everything with an iron hand. Classrooms were about 50 kids. The three Rs were well taught. Next came some history, a religion class and in the higher grades, Civics and Geography as well. Besides all that we had lunch and recess. One misstep or disobeyed order and you were whacked across the head with the ever-present book in Sister's hand. When the Corporal Offence was serious enough, your knuckles were bloodied with her ruler.

Now, I can't say for sure, if that made me a better person, but I had a new found respect for obeying orders from a higher authority. Somehow, we have to get back to that. I'm sure there are legions of teachers who, with years of pent up rage, would be in favor of school yard beheadings on every other Tuesday.

Many parents are cowed these days by the threat of Government interference in the management of their offspring. The kids today are smart enough now that they know which local government busybody to call if you deservedly smack him around.

What would have happened in your day if you disrespected an adult or your mother with the "F" word. They'd still be looking for your body. In third grade, me and a buddy stole a cement mixer carburetor from a nearby construction site. My buddy ratted me out and my dad had me by the ankles, banging my head on the concrete cellar floor. I quickly learned that cement mixer carburetors were off limits. To this day I haven't lifted another one.

How do we get the government and its politically correct idiocy out of our hair? It's ridiculous. Government has gotten control over how you raise your kids and now the school systems are hamstrung by PC dictums. The teacher should be an extension of your parental authority, not a PC bureaucrat. When my parents got wind of a teacher smacking me around, they doubled the thrashing just for good measure. Why did that stop? Every parent who wants to smack their disrespectful kid had better join me in electing candidates from the Independent Tea Party.

I'm disgusted with the products of today's schooling. The district I'm most familiar with lately, serves a step-grandchild, a six foot one, smart as a whip, hot tempered bad-mouth, that is on his way to an eventual date with the county lock-up. Yet nobody can discipline him. The school district is waiting way too long tossing him into a boot camp school. A kid without a diploma (not a GED) is always at the bottom of the list. The Military doesn't even want them today. Our permissive society, parents afraid to exact discipline and the misguided concept in today's curriculum, that everyone is equal, is bullcrap. They all have equal opportunity, but they are not all equal by a long shot.

Lower intellect is the only somewhat excusable trait in today's miserable and ridiculous educational score-card. When you first start up a computer application on your computer, you are usually presented with a window that gives credit to all the software engineering contributors who designed the software, a nice accolade for them. This manuscript has been created on an Adobe product called "In-Design" It is top of the line professional software. Paying attention to the "About" window reveals hundreds of software and hardware contributors to

Adobe's product. The disheartening factor here is that 30+% of the engineering minds that created this superb software are not American. I'll bet that 75% of them are here on a "Green Card" work visa. The list reads like attendees at a UN bar-be-que. Where are our engineers? Who do we blame?

How about —

▶ **Tenured teachers protected by unions?**

▶ **Politically correct society and school boards?**

▶ **Restricting school and parental discipline because one faction is out of control?**

▶ **Lack of consequences for failure?**

▶ **Curriculum managed politically?**

▶ **Low utilization of facilities (empty buildings at 3 pm)?**

▶ **Multi-ethnic language and curriculum?**

▶ **Curriculum with useless courses?**

▶ **Curriculum that leaves out important subjects in today's world.**

For instance, today the world in is conflict, not with Islamic teachings, but by those who pervert ancient fundamental parables to ferment terroristic fanatics who seem to have world dominance as their goal. However there are almost 20 broad categories worldwide, called religions, that define the beliefs of most of the planet. Ignoring their influence on the world we inhabit seems ridiculous, even today as one of them is trying to force its domination on the rest. Students not understanding these issues are poorly trained.

Our current president is an example of another vital aspect of a missing curriculum in today's education. He is a brilliant orator. Not that all his pronouncements are original or believable, but his delivery is what got him locked into the minds of his public. Not that all students will ever be able to emote with his evangelistic fervor, but in today's world few people are able to express themselves publicly. What a shame. High school students should be able to speak publicly.

To get an indication of how screwed up our education system is today, just watch an episode of the Tonight show, when Jay Leno interviews random victims on LA streets, called the "Jaywalking Allstars". These people shouldn't be allowed to vote. I'm against abortion, but in some instances, there might have been justification.

Social Security

Fund this important entitlement from the money collected by the Consumption tax and apportion a fixed percentage annually to the Trust Fund. Recall all the Bonds (IOUs) depleting it, till it is solvent. That way the fund is continually funded , not only by employed workers, but by everyone who buys something, including exported products.

Welfare

Handouts without work should be eliminated. Americans have been scammed for years by those who have learned how to work the system. Progress was made on this front during the Clinton Administration, but the problem still drains State coffers. Welfare is a way-of-life that lazy people (not all) gravitate to, because the rules are lax enough that whole generations have grown up without ever having worked for a living. Why should they? If you learn all the right things to say, you get an "Access" card with food stamp allotments and even cash on it monthly plus free medical for your little bastards. It's a free credit card. All you have to do is have illegitimate kids and never get married.

I am proposing that the parents are sterilized after the first bastard in order that they may join the universal Services. Every 18 year old should be enrolled in Civilian Service, or the military. The salary earned replaces whatever welfare support you might have gotten in the past and your work there is credited against your Universal military or Civilian Service requirement.

THE AMERICAN MARQUE

Tradition

It is a *historical fact* that this nation was founded with the notion that we are "One nation under God". We bow to those who are offended by that thought. Too bad. We are not forced, at least in the civilized world, to believe one way or another.

What is objected to in America is a perceived lack of separation of Church affairs from State affairs which has pushed the atheists and ACLU to litigate the issue. Political Correctness steps in and tries to soothe the nay-sayers feelings by forbidding open displays of religious beliefs in government. If tradition has been established by the annual display of a Christmas tree and Manger scene on the Courthouse lawn, that display is criticized by some who have no tradition of their own and therefore say they are offended. They could start a tradition that might endure if enough constituents agree and it's done properly. Blacks have endured and now Kwanza is an observed annual tradition.

Tradition is recognition of an event, a belief or an achievement that becomes part of who we are, over time. The sum of all these traditions represent a people as much as the geography they inhabit. A war memorial in the middle of the Mojave Desert has a white cross to represent the sacrifice of those who died in war to protect our traditions, yet the governing jurisdiction there hadn't the guts to honor those men and defy the ACLU and its Atheist. There is no Christ on that cross. A plywood box covers it today. That symbol, over time, has come to mean sacrifice. It's time our Congress clarified that symbol in law and reaffirm that our American traditions will remain, inviolate.

Religion

Since creation, as mankind began to reason for himself and to fend for himself, first by himself, then in tribes, kingdoms, nations and on and on till today, where this mankind of ours is surviving but in a less than satisfactory manner with outcomes OK for some, but not everyone — conflict prevails.

The Theory of Evolution and Creationism all refer to the same thing, the origins of mankind and his progress on this planet. They are one and the same thing, but just from different viewpoints. Consider for instance, the fact that the teachings that are espoused by organized religion are parables devised by ancient teachers to instruct the students of the time. They are interpretations of their own particular history and experiences, stories related to others so they could all follow the teacher's path to a perceived wellbeing. Parables are stories, created to teach by analogy the right way according to the teacher, an Apostle, Mullah, Rabbi or a Priest.

Keep in mind the viewpoint of these teachers. They were the "learned men" of their time, whose oratory gathered followers, who in turn began to live by their mentor's parables and teachings. The time is the antiquity of man.

There was precious little science other than learning how to start a fire or grow a bean. As centuries passed, science began to creep into man's evolution, hence the precision of ancient undertakings, like the mathematics used in designing and building pyramids.

As man's intellect evolved, so did his quest for discovery.

68

He began to look into the "how or why" of things. This was the beginning of independent inquiry leading to theoretical discovery, the "Evolution of Man" and all of today's scientific knowledge. In the abstract, mankind followed ancient parables to guide their everyday pursuits and followed scientific precepts when delving into "How does it work?"

Today's arguments neglect to include man's capacity to think in abstract terms and the absolutes of science within the same mind. Fundamentalist teachings should always be tempered with the thought that they were probably not meant to be anymore than generalizations. Did Moses part the Red Sea?

That parable is used in fundamental teaching to describe, in apocryphal terms, the march of the Jews to safety, driven by the Egyptian Pharaoh, waaaaaaay back when. I don't believe there was any science implied in that story. There probably was a drought and Moses got lucky. In the abstract, Moses was God's messenger.

The key to understanding the Religious mess our world is in today is in realizing that demigods are perverting ingrained Fundamental teachings, using them as a tool to further conflict and to pressure those who don't think for themselves into believing their religion wants them to take over everyone else's religion and that theirs is the only way. When I attended Catholic grammar school, the good Nuns taught that you weren't going to heaven if you were a Protestant. Thank God I wasn't one of them. Goodness sakes!

The basic need for religion, any religion or all religion for that matter, is to teach developing minds how to interact with others in a civilized and moral manner, *in today's world.* It really doesn't matter how you learned to "Do unto others as you would have them do unto you," as long as you learn it and live by it. You don't need an organized religion to learn and to follow that precept.

"Made in America"

We need a concerted effort to "Buy American" Every item for sale has a Country of Origin stamped on it somewhere. I'd like to see all purveyors make American Made items more prominent. All catalogs should list "Country of Origin" in every advertisement. Major retailers should prominently and proudly display that American Made fact. I'll bet that the retail industry will be pleasantly surprised at the result.

Not too many years ago I believe the Federal Government had required "Made in America" on all purchases. I remember back in the 1970s, the company I was working for at the time (Burroughs Corp.) was preparing a bid for some computer equipment for the State of New Jersey. It had a requirement to "Buy American", but there was a caveat that "elsewhere" was OK if there was no other source. In this case, I had to open up one of these computer systems and actually count all the computer chips not made in the US.

I realize that Free Trade Agreements changed the whole dynamic for the US and now we can't compete. Ruinous Union Contracts along with global trade rules put us way behind the 8-ball. When trade agreements were signed, union agreements should've been unsigned. All of the points I've mentioned in preceding pages should have been realized before giving away the business to the rest of the world.

Do you (fogeys) remember after WWII, when Japan was beginning to recover from fire bombing and "A" bombing, how their manufacturing was limited to toys made from old GI beer-cans, we supposed. With the exception of "I can't stop my damn Toyota" problem, their manufactured products have led the world in manufacturing quality, over time taking that trophy away from the Detroit mantle.

Taiwan has produced just about every chip invented for our electronic gadget lust, including most of our flat-panel TVs and cell-phones.

I remember when Zenith (remember that name) produced TV picture tubes in a Philadelphia suburb. No more.

I remember when Philco-Ford produced Ford radios and electronics, not far away from the Zenith plant. No more.

Before that merger, Philco produced stereos and TVs, radios and refrigerators right in Philadelphia at several different plants. No more.

Ethan Allen produced some of the finest furniture for American homes in Bradford, PA. My friend, Rich doesn't work there anymore. He's laid off. His plant is no more.

Bethlehem Steel in Allentown, PA is a vast rusty wasteland, as is the US Steel plant in Bristol, PA. No more.

The T-shirt on my back is made in Northern Marianis Islands! Where the hell is that? It's a good one too, made for Van Heusen — top quality. What happened to the clothing mills in Philadelphia? No more.

I'm a hypocrite. I'm preaching to the unwashed about buying American, but I don't have the money to not get the best bargain. Most of Wal-Mart's private-brand food products are as good as the name brands and they are 20% cheaper. I preach that we should shop at Small Town American stores, yet beer at Wal-Mart is a buck cheaper? I'm going to have to force my resolve to follow my preachings, before the financial reality of tomorrow's world catches up with me.

Because those who were in charge of America had no resolve, or at least no plan I was ever privy to, we've completely abandoned many of the things that made America, "America". We now have malls every mile or so, while other parts of the world are embracing what we've abandoned. We are now worshiping a Global Economy, a World Wide Wal-Mart. There's no identity in that.

I keep wondering why and how we've evolved into this non-American wasteland, trying to pin blame and to decide what to do to rectify this continent-wide blunder. The only logical explanation, is that we Baby Boomers had withdrawn in preparation for retirement at 55 or so and have allowed younger entrepreneurs and scions to redesign America into what they think it should be and should look like, based on their lack of what it was like — our America.

These are the future leaders of America I'm talking about. Are they the ones who are redesigning it all without the wisdom of what made America great? Are they making faster cars, higher definition, more Aps, more Gs and broader Boulevards when we don't really need them? Should we have let them destroy what the word America meant, and what the word America will mean forevermore? Everybody over 55 — baby boomers and me, are to blame. We've spent most of our later years, just planning to have a good retired time and to hell with working to keep the American Marque alive.

We need some adult minds to get off at the ninth hole and back into the action to lead the whipper-snappers down the right path — back to Grady. If you're under 55, you probably can't even spell "Wisdom", much less have any. The elite, yuppie, Manhattan mentality is not where most of adult America wants to be. I live in a trailer. If anybody knows where Grady is, call — pleeeease!

Lets get it back

We have to have a third Registered Political Party. Now is the time when the real American giant is waking from its slumber. The WOM (Wisdom of Age) Tea Party crowd has imbibed enough of the political pills forced through by legislators not controlled by us, but by some mysterious "Omega" world governance. Does anyone think Obama was smart enough and powerful enough to have engineered this Health Care swindle without behind the scenes orchestration way over our heads? Someone is pulling his strings.

We've just seen how easy it was to push through unwanted legislation when you have the power to twist arms, and the balls to bend, subvert or misuse rules. Up to now, we weren't paying much attention. Now we are.

Creating a new party with muscle is not an easy task, but there has never been a better time in my view to make it happen. The Tea Party people are united in their disgust with the way American politics has degenerated, but I don't yet see any real have a good retired time and to hell with working to keep the American Marque alive.

We need some adult minds to get off at the ninth hole and back into the action to lead the whipper-snappers down the right path — back to Grady. If you're under 55, you probably can't even spell "Wisdom", much less have any. The elite, yuppie, Manhattan mentality is not where most of adult America wants to be. I live in a trailer. If anybody knows where Grady is, call — pleeeease!

Lets get it back

We have to have a third Registered Political Party. Now is the time when the real American giant is waking from its slumber. The WOM (Wisdom of Age) Tea Party crowd has imbibed enough of the political pills forced through by legislators not controlled by us, but by some mysterious "Omega" world governance. Does anyone think Obama was smart enough and powerful enough to have engineered this Health Care swindle without behind the scenes orchestration way over our heads? Someone is pulling his strings.

We've just seen how easy it was to push through unwanted legislation when you have the power to twist arms, and the balls to bend, subvert or misuse rules. Up to now, we weren't paying much attention. Now we are.

Creating a new party with muscle is not an easy task, but there has never been a better time in my view to make it happen. The Tea Party people are united in their disgust with the way American politics has degenerated, but I don't yet see any real as good as the name brands and they are 20% cheaper. I preach that we should shop at Small Town American stores, yet beer at Wal-Mart is a buck cheaper? I'm going to have to force my resolve to follow my preachings, before the financial reality of tomorrow's world catches up with me.

Because those who were in charge of America had no resolve, or at least no plan I was ever privy to, we've completely abandoned many of the things that made America, "America". We now have malls every mile or so, while other parts of the world are embracing what we've abandoned. We are now worshiping a Global Economy, a World Wide Wal-Mart. There's no identity in that.

I keep wondering why and how we've evolved into this non-American wasteland, trying to pin blame and to decide what to do to rectify this continent-wide blunder. The only logical explanation, is that we Baby Boomers had withdrawn in preparation for retirement at 55 or so and have allowed younger entrepreneurs and scions to redesign America into what they think it should be and should look like, based on their lack of what it was like — our America.

These are the future leaders of America I'm talking about. Are they the ones who are redesigning it all without the wisdom of what made America great? Are they making faster cars, higher definition, more Aps, more Gs and broader Boulevards when we don't really need them? Should we have let them destroy what the word America meant, and what the word America will mean forevermore? Everybody over 55 — baby boomers and me, are to blame. We've spent most of our later years, just planning to direction towards a workable plan to begin the metamorphosis into an awakened giant – and real choice for Americans.

What I am hearing is that the Republicans don't want a third party, because they are afraid it will take away votes in their perceived rout of the Democrat majority in the 2012 elections. If they do win in 2012, we'll still have two deadlocked parties using every known trick or ploy to win an issue. The Republicans are not much better. They just weren't in charge this time. We have to have a third choice to force negotiation.

Americans who are disgusted with this mysterious, self-serving government we've allowed to happen, should welcome the chance to have a moderating voice that may help mitigate "Congress-gate" as we've come know it.

Get involved. Lets get everybody who thinks we really do need a change, to help create our new "Independent Tea Party" in time for 2012.

NOW!